Advance Praise

Cynthia Reese encourages us to develop self insight about the strange and shaky nature of fear, and if we cling to our fears how self limiting fear can be. Reese calls on her reader to gain inspiration from Scripture when faced with decisions that seem big and scary. This book encourages us to not wait for life to happen, but take charge, taking new steps toward fulfilling our dreams.

-**Janette E. Borel**, Master of Arts in Organizational Communications, College of Professional Studies, Regis University, CO

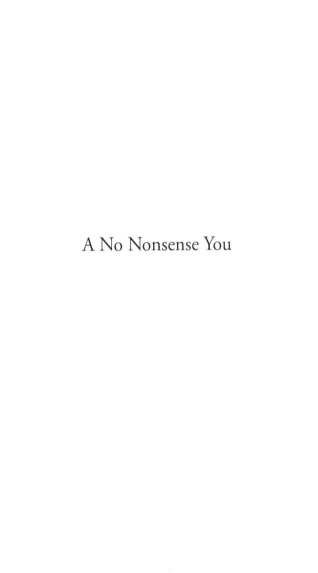

A No Nonsense You

A No Nonsense *you*

Seven Simple Steps to Find and Fulfill Your Destiny

DR. CYNTHIA REESE

NEW YORK

LONDON • NASHVILLE • MELBOURNE • VANCOUVER

A No Nonsense You

Seven Simple Steps to Find and Fulfill Your Destiny

Published in New York, New York, by Morgan James Publishing in partnership with Difference Press. Morgan James is a trademark of Morgan James, LLC. www.MorganJamesPublishing.com

ISBN 9781642790627 paperback
ISBN 9781642790634 eBook
Library of Congress Control Number: 2018941626

Cover Design by:
Heather Kirk
www.GFSstudio.com

Interior Design by:
Chris Treccani
www.3dogcreative.net

Morgan James is a proud partner of Habitat for Humanity Peninsula and Greater Williamsburg. Partners in building since 2006.

Get involved today! Visit
MorganJamesPublishing.com/giving-back

Dedication

My reasons for writing and striving daily to practice what I preach are for my daughters, Zakiya and Zalika. My mom, Ethel who gave me the book's title. Siblings: Gwendolyn, Susie, Pamela, Gregory, Rosa, and Clifford. In loving memory of my brother Zerion (1965-2018) and grandparents, Mary (1923 – 2000) and Paul (1919-2000).

Also, remaining family members, people who have crossed my path all over the world that have allowed me to serve and love; have served and loved me, and all females, particularly single moms. I pray someday this book and ministry bring God glory and women pride in being a part of it all. I humbly thank you and I love you very much, amen.

Table of Contents

Introduction

Do you have something on the inside knocking to get outside? Is being a jack of all trades keeping you a master of none? You know you have the gift of gab, can create interest, attract others to the scene, but have no idea of the one message to master? Do you fear – fear? It is okay to have some fear, but it is not okay to let fear have you. Find and fulfill your destiny! To find and fulfill your destiny, it is necessary to take the following seven powerful steps – FULFILL your way to the greatness in You!

Fear must go now
Unleash your passion

Like being YOU
Follow the signs
Instill your values
Learn from the greats
Look, listen, and leap!

As I travel through my journey, sharing personal experiences of FULFILL, I have helped many women find and fulfill their destiny. It's now time for me to help You!

Chapter 1
Fear Must Go Now

Each of us has a call to action in our lives. Some refer to this as our purpose or destiny. Moses was called to action by God to lead the Israelites out of Egypt. After crossing the Red Sea and in the wilderness, the people began mumbling, grumbling, complaining, and making gods of gold. Moses was getting "beat down", feeling afraid for them and helpless. The good news is, he knew where his help came from. Moses did not engage in a pity party, he did not go to God in prayer asking for something amiss (wrong or out of place), like the man James talks about in James 1:23-25, *a hearer, not doer of the Word, that looks in the mirror, turns away and forgets what he saw.* He went to God in praise! In Exodus 33:18, Moses asked, Lord show me Your glory! He showed us what to do when the enemy rises, making us feel afraid and helpless. Proverbs 3:6 says *in all thy ways acknowledge him, and He shall direct thy paths.*

The Word of God reveals His glory as a noun (a thing) and verb (an action) throughout the Bible from Genesis to Revelation. Glory in man's thinking, as a noun, is high renown or honor won by notable achievements, magnificence; great beauty. God's thinking of glory is goodness (character – one of the fruit of The Holy Spirit). In Exodus 33:19, God said to Moses, *I will let my goodness pass before thee.* Our thinking contrasts (is different from) God's. In Isaiah 55:9, The Lord says, *as the heavens are higher than the earth, so are my ways higher than your ways and my thoughts than your thoughts.* According to Ephesians 3:20, *God is able to do exceeding abundantly above all that we ask or think, according to the power that worketh in us,* therefore, when we rely on God's power to accomplish a task, fear must go now, for we are not relying on ourselves, and failure is not an option. When we embark on a task or goal to meet, it matters who we pair up with. In Matthew 18:20, The Lord says, *where two or three are gathered together in my name, there am I in the midst of them.* When we pray together in Jesus' name, God's power is poured out in ways exceeding abundantly above that we ask or think.

Glory as a verb by man's thinking, is to take pride or pleasure in. To an extent, if we are not careful, it can be carnal – adhering to flesh. In 1 John 2:16, the Lord lets us know, the pride of life is of the world. Also, in Exodus 33:19, God says *I will proclaim the name of The Lord before you and be gracious and show mercy!*

In other words, The Lord says <u>I will declare, I will show divine grace, and I will make it visible!</u> You won't have to tell a Soul. Everybody will know it. Everybody will see it! I heard Les Brown describe fear as "false expectations appearing real". To me, that defines an illusion, something unreal appearing real. When God does something it is not an illusion, it is real. God gives each of us revelation of who He is according to our belief and His grace. We can actually replace belief – with faith. Jesus put it this way in Luke 17:6 – *if you have faith the size of a mustard seed you can say to this sycamine tree, be plucked up by the root and planted in the sea, and it shall obey you.* Of course, this is a metaphor for a problem. Get rid of it from the root, in Jesus name! God doesn't treat symptoms nor puts bandages over them. Pluck it up from the root, never to return. I heard a preacher ask one time about the sycamine tree – are you sick of yours? Then responded – 'cause I'm sick-a-mine! I have learned to measure my faith in a couple of ways: 1. For all I trust Him, and 2. For all I thank Him. When believing and trusting God, which by the way is ongoing, not just situational, is the solid foundation from which I stand. On Christ the solid rock I stand, all other ground is sinking sand. I thank Him in advance knowing He will provide for He already knows what I need and want. In John 15:7, Jesus said *if you abide in me, and my words abide in you, you shall ask what you will, and it will be done unto you.* Fear must go now! Lord show me your glory in this fear. I will not allow fear to keep me from accomplishing my goals. I will not allow fear to rob me of my happiness. I will not allow fear to prevent me from creating abundant wealth!

Fear causes a sense of helplessness. If we back up to Exodus 32:9, The Lord said to Moses, *I have seen these people and it is a stiffnecked people.* Stiffnecked – stubborn, unyielding, obstinate. Rebuke/admonish that negativity, look to Jesus and declare, **Lord, show me Your glory in this situation, pain, anger, doubt, finances, whatever the circumstance.** God loves every boy and girl as He does every man and woman. I say to the youth – if you are challenged with a subject, have a mean or difficult teacher, pray for yourself by saying Lord show me Your glory, and pray for your teacher by saying, Lord show my teacher Your glory. Jesus allowed Himself to be beaten all night, nailed to a rugged cross, died, and rose early one Sunday morning with all power in His hands so we could declare, **Lord show me your glory!** Know that God's glory is His presence in that endeavor, circumstance, or whatever you are asking, and when God shows up, fear must go now!

Some fear is good for us. Many years ago, I found myself madly in love with a man that obviously loved himself more than me, and I was afraid of my heart getting broken, so I began focusing on ways to protect my heart. It was very difficult admitting to myself this predicament, for I wanted to believe there was something I could do to change it. Of course there wasn't, for when a man loves himself, he loves himself. He asked me one afternoon, "Cynthia why do you like me so much?" That should have been an indication to me just how one-sided the relationship was, but no – me, looking through my rose colored eyes, began thinking how to answer him. I hadn't been asked that before. As I opened my mouth to answer, he interrupted by telling me "don't answer now, tell me later." I was driving, thinking about my answer, and it came to me in the form of a poem:

Why do I like You?

I like your style, smile, masculinity

Tall lean body, charisma, sexuality

I like the way you think, blink, talk

The smooth even glide of your walk

I'm saying I like you, and I do

But in reality baby, I want to be
loved by you!

I scribbled it on a piece of paper, stopped at a store, bought a nice card, wrote it in the card, and gave it to him that night. He was speechless. I wrongly thought my mission had been accomplished. When I began seeing that it wasn't going where I thought it should, I started pulling back, cried a lot, focused on work, and eventually, it fizzled out.

The experience of loving someone more than myself, brought out the fear of rejection; a fear some find hard to overcome. Rejection that is not faced head-on and conquered may become crippling. Prayer is paramount in overcoming rejection. The assurance of Jesus' love for me is irreplaceable. We must remember in 2 Timothy 1:7 that God has not given us a spirit of fear. He has given us *love, power, and a sound mind.*

When I rose above the fear of rejection and made my true feelings known to him and myself, I realized how important it is, that fear must go now! I was then able to rechannel my energy inward (on my goal), focus on my destiny, and not let fear rob me of it. Fear must go now to find and FULFILL your destiny.

Chapter 2
Unleash Your Passion
Undo the Power and Guilt of Yesterday

Upset the Set-up!

Have you ever walked into a room and sensed adversity? Would you call this a trap the enemy has set? A fiery dart being thrown? It is a set-up! Have you gone home in a good mood…met a situation that SNATCHED the rug from under you? Would you call this a trap the enemy has set? A fiery dart being thrown?

It is a set-up! Have you been given a speaking assignment by the Lord and your mind goes blank as you approach the lectern? Would you call this a trap the enemy has set? A fiery dart being thrown? It is a set-up!

The Lord is saying to us – Ladies, it is time to UPSET the SET-UP!
Weak things….set-up
Mighty things…set-up
Fear that causes doubt…set-up
Low self-esteem…set-up

Joseph

Genesis Chapter 50 continues the story of Joseph, a young man who was favored over his brothers by their father. The father, Jacob, loved him so much that he gave Joseph a coat of many beautiful colors. Joseph's brothers had a plot to kill him, resulting from jealousy and envy of their father's favor for him; but God intervened and they sold Joseph into captivity. While in Egypt, a captive, The Lord caused a famine to come upon the land, and his brothers **had** to come to him for food. Genesis 50:20 reveals Joseph's attitude when he realized his brothers were among the many there for food; *What the devil means for evil (**set-up**) God turns into your good (**upset**).* Joseph showed kindness to his brothers and all their offsprings. His family remained in Egypt with him and were well cared for. Joseph did something very difficult – he showed kindness to people that did him wrong, very wrong, without provocation from him. He turned the other cheek, the power and guilt of yesterday were undone through love!

Moses

When The Lord showed me Moses, He showed me a glass with water to the mid-point. Since it wasn't clear why The Lord showed me water, I began to pray and The Lord placed

Moses' name before me. Upon researching Moses' name, I found that it comes from the name Mashah (since he was born a Hebrew) which means to draw out. When his mother placed him in the river, he fell into the hands of the enemy of his people. This could have been a glass half empty situation. In other words, a negative situation (**set-up**). Pharaoh, in Exodus 1:22 issued an order for all Hebrew boys to be killed. However, The Lord intervened and Moses was found by Pharaoh's daughter. She named him Moses, which in Egyptian means river-god. Pharaoh's daughter believed a son had been sent to her by the river-gods. In Exodus 2:10 we read, *And she called his name Moses: and she said, Because I drew him out of the water* (**upset**). God is so awesome that He placed Moses's sister in the right place at the right time, saw Pharoah's daughter rescue him, but stepped forward and asked for the job of getting a Hebrew woman to nurse the baby! The story gets sweeter – his sister took their mother to Pharaoh's daughter, and she is hired to nurse *her* son; to bond with him and be together daily.

Paul

Formerly known as Saul, a great persecutor of the people of God **(set-up)**, whom the Lord transformed into a great apostle **(upset)**. 1 Corinthians 1:27 clarifies Paul's transformation to me: *But God hath chosen the foolish things of the world to confound the wise; and God hath chosen the weak things of the world to confound the things which are mighty.* Saul's persecutions are told in Acts 8. He was about to sign Stephen's death certificate, (as we would call it today) after he was stoned to death, and also had men and women of the church throughout the region were thrown into prison at his command. Those affected were in Jerusalem, Judea, and Samaria.

Jonah

The enemy used Jonah as he has used many of us, I'm sure. He used Jonah against **himself**. Through disobedience, Jonah was **set-up**. In chapter 1 The Lord instructs Jonah to go preach to the people in Nineveh as a warning to their wrong doings, but Jonah went to Joppa with intentions to take sail into Tarshish instead. I perceive that Jonah's heart was in doing what he wanted, not what God wanted.

We women especially get used in this manner all too often. Jeremiah 17:9 warns *The heart is deceitful above all things, and desperately wicked: who can know it?* However, we meet a man, he is down on his luck, living with a relative, no vehicle, no job presently, but is so very tall, dark, and handsome. Not to mention, fine as wine! We get to know him, fall for him, decide to help him, when we should stop to realize God's order of things with Adam and Eve. In chapter 1 of Genesis, God created the heaven, earth, beasts of the fields and birds of the air. He creates light separating from darkness and established the seasons. He created trees to bear fruit, vines to produce vegetables, seeds as nuts, separated the waters – fresh and salt. Then He created man, breathed life into Adam. In chapter 2 of Genesis, God decided it was not good for man to be alone, put Adam to sleep, took a rib from him, formed Eve and brought her to him. Ladies, Philippians 4:19 should come to mind right now, *But my God shall supply all your need according to His riches in glory by Christ Jesus.* Let's take notice, Eve did not need to help Adam get up on his feet when God gave her to him. God had created everything they would need. We think it is the heart we're following, which is deceitful, but we are following the flesh **(set-up)**. It's time to UPSET the SET-UP on the goals you have to achieve, projects to finish, classes to complete, papers to publish, and books to write!

The enemy may strike our physical bodies; but his main workplace is in our **minds**! One powerful tool he uses against us is discernment, by invoking self-doubt **(set-up)**. We may use the gift of discernment to defeat that trick **(upset)**. I read something written by Charles Stanley on discernment that helped me to understand this wonderful gift that I will share in simple terms, to help you in relation to everyday life:

Discernment between good and evil. General principles related to right and wrong. When God breathed the breath of life into us, He breathed consciousness into us. The ability to distinguish between right and wrong is inherent, a strong gut feeling, a soft whisper in our minds, an intuition, a sense of, all attributes of God's character. Genesis 1:27 says we were created in His own image.

Discernment between what is real and what is an illusion. I had the pleasure of attending a theatrical Peter Pan performance, with Indians on stage. I wondered – real Indians or not, for if I looked closely, there were fish lines extending from the ceiling to them, perhaps. I pondered, is it live or Memorex? I recall that phrase from previous Memorex TV ads in past years. Many times, situations come up that overwhelm us, for we forget Peter's forewarning in 1 Peter 5:8, our adversary seeks whom he can devour. The enemy sends things to appear bigger than they are, like bulldogs barking but have no teeth to bite. Illusions. God will show us what is real. Paul says in 2 Corinthians 2:11 that *unless Satan gets an advantage over us, we are not ignorant of his devices.*

Discernment between what is good and what is best. A poem I taught my daughters at an early age: good better best, never let it rest until good becomes better, and better becomes best. I now look at this differently, for in Genesis 1:31 *God saw everything that He had made, and, behold, it was very good.* James 1:17 states *every* *good gift and every perfect gift is from above.* Good is divine, from God. Upping the ante to best is from man. Of course, we strive to do our best. I am learning more daily the significance of fulfilling 1 Corinthians 10:31, *whatsoever ye do, do all to the glory of God.* We put extra pressure reaching for external things we've been taught. We have inside us a barometer that measures our mark. With a heart to please the Lord, a servant's heart, we will be led to the level of achievement that is predestined for us. Difficulties come oftentimes without notice; but with the mindset to do everything to the glory of God, doing what is good will eventually become second nature. Pressure gone.

Discernment between our desires and God's plan. Many women have made this common mistake when it comes to relationships, in that we compromise our standards. This goes back to the example I shared in the Jonah story. God's plan for Eve was to be Adam's companion and help mate. God's plan was for them to be fruitful and multiply. Adam could not do it alone. We tend to take on additional tasks on our own. Another example that comes to mind is a story of a man who was a Christian with a son that had his heart set on being an actor. The father's plan was for his son to be a doctor. The son, not wanting to disappoint his father, began the journey to becoming a doctor. He enrolled in a drama class while in college and from there, became a Christian actor. The father was pleased with the son's evolution, and saw acting as a way to bring glory to God. A doctor is instrumental in physical healing, and acting produces entertainment, which is instrumental in mental healing. The father saw God's plan for his son, not just his plan. We need to get in the habit of pursuing the things that are naturally a desire within; believing it is God speaking to us, then we will do what we're supposed to and become who we are supposed to.

The sports arena has given a very clear picture of taking the negative and turning into the positive. Outside the sports arena, the word **upset** is treated as a negative. To upset is to flip over or to capsize. In the sports arena upset is to defeat unexpectedly! We can defeat circumstances thrown in our paths to trip us, intending to defeat us, and cast down our dreams by deciding today to upset the set-up. Decide today and actually stop reacting to circumstances. Take action, take the driver's seat and navigate through what is necessary to achieve the outcome you want, not that which is wanted of you by external demands. What you are supposed to be and doing is in you, it's in us. God put it there. We do not have to stretch ourselves into multiple tasks, being overly stressed, burned out, and miserable to achieve greatness. Malachi puts it this way in Malachi 3:10, *I will open the windows of heaven and pour out a blessing you will not have room* *enough to receive.* A blessing. Stop being a jack of all trades, become master of one.

You upset the set-up when you charter the course of life, unleash your passion to find and FULFILL Your destiny!

Chapter 3
Like Being You

There are several sayings out there to help us like and love ourselves, such as, *like the skin you're in, I like being me, it's all about me,* are a few. Truth be told, they are all positive and make me feel good saying them. Speaking positive affirmations, such as these sayings, to myself helped me to find and fulfill my destiny by seeing more good in me, and less self doubt. Many have shared how they are able to find and fulfill their destiny with the increased energy positive affirmations like these fuel. You can also. The thing to be careful of is where your intention is, where your heart is. For myself, I had to start from the inside first. People will always tell you how your skin is looking. That's the external/physical attraction. It is true – attractive people attract people. The challenge is getting the inside right for you with you, bearing the raw truth only between you and the Lord in prayer. My grandmother would say, *have a little talk with Jesus.* Jesus says for us to cast our cares or concerns on Him, for He cares for us in 1 Peter 5. Knowing that we are loved just as we are is encouraging. Courage is needed as we seek to find and fulfill our destiny. More often than not, that courage has to come from within. James gives the clearest instructions in James 1: 25 *whoso looks into the perfect law of liberty, and continues therein, he being not a forgetful hearer, but a doer of the work, this man shall be blessed in his deed.* We have it within us and by getting close to The Lord, filled with The Holy spirit, we cannot fail. There is no failure in God and I can do all things through him who gives me strength.

In exercising my love for the Lord, I show love for others and myself. *JOY – Jesus, Others, Yourself.* I remain conscious of self-condemning statement such as as *why am I so stupid? That was dumb, why did I do it? I knew better than that.* None of them are true; they are wiles of the devil. When a negative thought enters into our minds, it is very important to rethink it on the positive. I am a reasonable thinking person, let me look at this for a better way it could be done, and let me look at this and learn. We must remember that the fight is not with the world or darkness of outside forces, flesh and blood. We wrestle with spiritual powers of high places, our minds. We must renew our minds by replacing negative condemning thoughts with positive, loving thoughts. Self-anger is another wile of the devil. Have you ever had the thought, I'm so mad at myself right now? That is a terrible thought, for anger usually provokes negative actions. What would I do to myself in a moment of anger? What have I done to someone else in a moment of anger and regretted it later? Anger hurts. Abuse results from unresolved anger. There are victims of abuse walking around right now with a lot of anger bottled up inside with no idea where it comes from or why it is there. Abused children have bottled up anger resulting from the helplessness felt towards the power the abuser (an adult) has over them, and no one to protect them. More often than not, the abuser is supposed to be the protector, the one to give and teach love, nurture. Bottled up anger can lead to both physical and mental problems. Stress, high blood pressure, heart problems, depression, isolation are a few. Unresolved anger destroys relationships, beginning with self, which can lead to another type of abuse, self-destructive behavior. Drinking alcohol excessively, using illicit drugs, smoking, practicing promiscuity are detrimental to the body, mind, and relationships - life destroying behaviors. Like fear, not all anger is bad or harmful. Some anger is useful and good for us. For example, if a student gets angry over a test grade, studies harder, gets a better grade on the next test, anger served the student well. Someone that gets angry because the bulk of their earnings go to debt versus savings, devises a budget to start getting out of debt and saving more re-channels anger to a positive. Unresolved anger feeds un-forgiveness, which hurts physically and mentally. Unresolved anger focuses on the bad, which could turn our thoughts into worry, causing ulcers or high blood pressure (physically) and anxiety or depression (mentally). When we like who we are, we see the good in ourselves, and that enables us to see the good in others. Seeing the good in ourselves catapults us to want the best, and we achieve that when we set out to find and fulfill our destiny. **The torment of un-forgiveness and the benefits of forgiveness**

Matthew 18 verses 28-35 teach us on the torments of un-forgiveness. Let's begin with the prefix "un":

- Indicates not or contrary to. For example, un-happy.
- Indicates reversal of an action. For example, un-lock.
- Indicates release or removal from. For example, un-yoke. Sin or self-destructive behavior puts a yoke on us. The Holy Spirit removes the yoke! The Holy Spirit teaches us love, for others and ourselves.

In verse 28, the servant went out and found a fellow servant that owed him a hundred pence. One pence is $17. He laid hands on him, grabbed him by the throat saying *pay me that you owe.* In my mind's eye, I visualize this servant being punched and choked over $17. They must've been living in an economy like ours today! The small amount of $17 may look like $1700 depending on whose eyes you're seeing through. Clearly, the servant laying hands on the other is un-repented as many Jews were in those days for they felt their ancestry entitled them to the kingdom of God. This scenario is a clear case of brother-to-brother, servant to fellow servant. There are several elements in this encounter:

1. A new freedom – power (one over the other).
2. A small debt – with possibility of payment. Mercy was asked for, no mercy was shown. He cast his fellow servant in prison.

3. A reckoning – how many of us are aware that what we do today matters in eternity?

The servant was blinded to his surroundings. He gave no thought of whether he was seen or not. 1 Corinthians 4:5 lets us know that when the Lord comes, He will bring to light the hidden things of darkness. We paraphrase that by saying *what's done in the dark will come to light*. As a result of the servant's un-forgiveness, he was delivered to the tormentors. The tormentors were the jailers who had charge of prisoners and who also tormented them when ordered to do so. You see, un-forgiveness leaves us to torment. Self-torment is manifested as alcoholism, drug addiction, depression, promiscuity and other self-destructive behavior. The torments of un-forgiveness can lead to violence or murder. Scripture puts it this way – as I paraphrase Joshua 5:13, he asked, are you for us or against us? I ask myself this question so my aim is to be a friend, not enemy to myself. In Romans, chapter 8, Apostle Paul calls self-destructive behavior as *being carnally minded which is death, but to be spiritually minded is life and peace.* Peace in our hearts and minds free up our thoughts to focus on ways to find and fulfill our destiny. Now let's look at the benefits of forgiveness.

In Matthew 18:21, Peter asks Jesus the question, *how oft* or how often shall I forgive my brother? Jesus answers with a big number, 70 times 7 equaling 490, painting a picture – indefinitely. No boundaries or ceiling. No caps. I recommend applying this principle with ourselves. We need to be quick to forgive ourselves as mercifully as we forgive others. Jesus goes on to teach a lesson in contrast. A servant owing a debt to a king. Ten thousand talents in gold, one talent is $29,085 – 10,000 talents of gold are $290,850,000. In silver, one talent is $1,920, 10,000 talents of silver would be $19,200,000. This explains why the king's order when the servant was unable to pay – sell him, his wife, children, and all that he has for payment to be made. There are several elements in this encounter:

1. A king and a servant, a ruler and a subordinate.
2. A great debt without possibility of repayment.
3. Mercy was asked for – benefits were received: compassion (king's), cancellation of debt, promise (servant's to pay in verse 20), cancellation of debt.

God cancels all debts for penitent sinners as this king did for his servant. Jesus taught us to pray in saying *forgive us our debt as we forgive our debtors, forgive us our trespass as we forgive our trespassers* in Luke 11:4. God demands fair treatment between Christians. God will not forgive unless man forgives his brother. All issues of sin and righteousness come from the heart. Matthew 6:21 states, *for where your treasure is, there will your heart be also.* The greatest act of un-forgiveness led to Calvary's mountain… the greatest benefit was on Calvary's cross. The bottom line is un-forgiveness is the manifestation of unbelief. We must believe that we are worth forgiving to ourselves and prevent self-destructive behavior, and replace it with self-respect and self-esteem.

I was working on fear and anger within myself years ago to let go of past hurts in order to forgive the persons that had imposed those emotions and found the two, fear and anger, are related. I call them cousins. Many emotions had been buried for years and years for I was not allowed to express myself, being a child that was abused. I've read many self-help books and attended conferences, classes, counseling, of course church, and developed a process that has served and continues to serve me well, and find it interesting that it spells out fear. I decided and recommend you decide to:

Feel what you're feeling. Don't deny your feelings, let yourself feel, as hard as it is, that's a necessary step in a positive direction and healing.

Express to yourself what you feel. It's okay to tell yourself that this hurts so much, this hurts me to the core, and this hurts very deeply. It is also okay to let tears flow, male and female both need to sometimes shed tears. Deep cries if necessary, multiple times crying for the same painful experience or situation are alright.

Allow the pain. It will not help to mask it with taking a drink, which may lead to another, then another…you get the picture, for the same applies for taking a drug or smoke, or satisfying a sexual urge. Taking a walk in a safe place away from traffic can help, or talking to a confidant can be soothing.

Release the pain. After feeling, expressing, allowing it, there is absolutely no reason for it to hang around and fuel un-forgiveness. Letting the pain go will free that space for better feelings, joy, happiness, love, community, and high self-esteem. You will like being you for you will be in control, which is a nice spot to be in! Forgiveness takes place within and outside which means when we forgive ourselves, we can forgive others. In church, we hear *let go and let God*. That means to let go of past hurts, anger, abuse, anything that is causing negativity in you, and let God heal the inner you, and the outer you will be exuberant. Energy increases, the mind opens up, and good things begin to happen or manifest.

After accomplishing the FEAR process of going within myself and seeing what was there that I did not want in there, I wrote this poem:

As I See Myself

I like your style, smile, mentality

Fine womanly body, charisma,
sexuality

Your ability to endure

Not always having to be sure

Your maternal capabilities

Providing your daughters' securities

Men see you as forceful

Bossy and thick

Not understanding your inwardness

Tenderness, softness, unlike brick

I see you as sleek, chic, stunning

Knowledgeable, sharing, caring, and
cunning

Persistency and determination are
yours

Success is imminent as you journey
through

Opened doors

You're a lot of fun hun

A one of a kind girl

Enjoying life in this world

I love you Cynthia, I do, I do, I do

Plus you have two wonderful
daughters who

Adore and love you, too!

Writing this poem to me was the beginning of a turning point for me. It catapulted me to shift my focus. I began assessing the amount of energy I was exerting in others, in lieu of myself. I told you earlier of a relationship I was in with a man I felt was not in love with me to the extent I was with him. I began looking at the amount of energy I was putting into relationships realistically, not through rose colored glasses. Relationships with friends that were not reciprocal, I was being used for various reasons. Relationships with relatives, also not reciprocal, also were being used for the other person's agenda, where my only agenda was the relationship; I was in search of love from others when the real love had to come from me to me first, after The Lord. With the renewing of my mind in process, I began developing an attitude of believing in myself, truly. I began focusing on doing what is in me, not what is in my circumstances. Little did I realize that a separation had taken place. I was separated from The Lord. Apostle Paul asks the question in Romans 8:35, *Who shall separate us from the love of Christ*? Not who shall keep Christ from loving us, but who shall keep us from loving Him? *Shall tribulation, or distress, or persecution, or famine, or nakedness, or peril, or sword*? At that times, for me, it was distress. I was in distress of being a single parent, earning enough to support my children and me, earning a college degree, being loved as much as I was loving others. I had my affections focused on the wrong things, in error, for I'd learned to *set my affections on things above, not on things on the earth*, Colossians 3:2. This is the true idea, for the things listed here might affect men, but not Christ. If we will not permit them to affect our love for Christ, then we are safe from all danger of backsliding:

- tribulation – distress, affliction
- distress – to trouble
- persecution – the act of pursuing with harassing or the state of being harassed. (You are harassing someone or someone is harassing you).
- famine – hunger, want of food
- nakedness – lightly clad, or without proper clothing
- peril – exposure to danger
- sword – an offensive weapon with an iron or bronze blade. It is especially lethal when it is two-edged.

Paul continues in verses 38-39 with *for I am persuaded, that neither death* (loss of life), *nor life* (natural life), *nor angels* (a messenger of God, or a messenger of the devil*), nor principalities* (dominions of princes or rulers), *nor powers* (mights, strengths, authorities), *nor things present* (seen), *nor things to come* (unseen), *nor height* (elevation, measure of stature, *nor depth* (deep places, abyss, how low I go), *nor any other creature* (humanity individually or collectively or an animal), *shall be able to separate us from the love of God, which is Christ Jesus our Lord.* This affirmation is sealed with a promise in verse 37, *Nay, in all these things, we are more than conquerors through Him that loved us.* This means we are more than able to quit smoking. More than able to quit drinking. More than able to provide for our children. Jesus is more than a man that was hung on the cross. Jesus is more than a man that had a crown of thorns on His head. He is a Saviour that lives in us. We must keep the right focus and not allow ourselves be dragged down the path of distress, which is a path of self-destruction. Of course, relationships are important and necessary. We were created to be in community. Remember, in Genesis, The Lord saw that it was not good for man to be alone after creating Adam, so He put Adam asleep, took a rib and created Eve for him.

I asked myself, whose life are you living? In answering this question to myself, I consciously decided to choose my life. You may ask, what life did you previously have, Cynthia? I had the life of my circumstances, developed through the unconscious observation of others' lives. Education was always encouraged in our culture of mostly agriculture laborers raising large families. It was commonplace for children to be put to work as soon as they were able to stand and walk on their own two feet. Most adults did not have the luxury of a high school education, for the vicious cycle had not been broken. African American youth did not have opportunities of paper routes, clerical jobs in grocery stores or downtown offices. There was never talk of it. The advice given was, stay in school, get your education so you won't have to do this the rest of your life. I did not realize as a child the adults were battered by their circumstances.

I chose to love my life. Haven't you heard someone say, I am happy to be alive? Or, I love life? Do you love your life, I ask? You can. I choose living, not just existing, moseying through without purpose or direction. With this conscious choice, every facet is thought through, every relationship is hand-picked, and every day is appreciated. I don't say this as an extremist; I say it with focus, with intent. Will you take a moment every day and ponder this thought…am I going to love life or love my life? My answer is, *if it's to be, it's up to me.* I must find and fulfill my destiny; you can too, when you like being You!

Chapter 4
Follow The Signs

Jesus knew as humans we would require the physical, the natural. He told the nobleman with a sick son in Matthew 4:48, *Except you see signs and wonders, you will not believe.* The nobleman was in Cana of Galilee where Jesus turned water into wine at the feast, so having seen Jesus perform a miracle, He saw a sign and believed that his son could be healed; however, remember, prophet Isaiah already told us our ways are not His (Jesus') ways.

In this instance Jesus chose to take the man's faith to another level. Jesus spoke the healing, He did not physically go to the son. Jesus told the nobleman *your son lives, go your way.* The nobleman believed what The Lord spoke and went his way. When he reached home, his son was well. He asked those present when did the fever leave his son? They responded the seventh hour yesterday and the father realized it was the same time he'd spoken to Jesus. Imagine if the nobleman had not taken Jesus at His word, not believed He spoke truth, and just left?

A fictional story I heard Will Smith talk about is The Alchemist, where a young shepherd goes on a quest for his treasure. Obstacles got in his path but he made the best of each situation until he actually met the alchemist. He was told the obstacles were signs and he did well following them. My take away from the story is to make negatives into positives. Negatives are trials, tribulations; Apostle Paul makes it plain in Romans 5:1-5. Paul explains the basis for us being justified is through our faith. Paul says that *we glory in tribulations also: knowing that tribulation works patience, and patience experience, and experience hope: and hope makes not ashamed; because the love of God is shed abroad in our hearts by the Holy Ghost which is given to us.* Haven't you heard, *trials come to make us stronger?* With developed patience, gained experience, keeping hope alive, and accepting the love of God, we will exude strength.

Signs and wonders are around us more than we realize, for we don't always recognize them. A recent experience for me in following the signs to find and fulfill my destiny is the writing of this book to serve others. I could only see writing my research paper and graduating, finishing the journey of my final higher degree and becoming Dr. Cynthia. The process was becoming more challenging and discouraging.

The process was consuming so much of my time, it was not enjoyable at all. It was a gigantic chore. I began praying, asking God to show me a sign of my path to destiny. I had no idea what I would do after graduating. Out of the blue one day I received an email inviting me to a session on writing a book that *makes a difference*. I responded, and here we are.

Signs, when followed, have a way of directing or redirecting us to God's plan for our lives – our true destiny. I have joy in writing. Joy in serving. I am on the right path, following the signs to find and fulfill my destiny and you can too!

Chapter 5
Instill Your Values Not Other Peoples' Values

Back to the Basics

Proverbs 31: 25-31

Chapter 31 of Proverbs is a lesson taught by a woman – a mother, through prophetically speaking/teaching her son, the king, King Lemuel.

Friends and sisters be reminded that in Old Testament days, women were for the most part, second class citizens. It was irregular for a king to be approached by a woman. Therefore, a king being counseled by a woman was unheard of.

However, through Solomon's pen, the Lord shows the wisdom of this woman's approach to the king by first humbling him down as her son – son of her womb, son of her vows. Then, she voices her concerns for the king!

Would you agree – regardless of our earthly greatness, in the kingdom of God, we are first sons and daughters?

Next, the wise woman of God, the king's mother, gets **back to the basics** beginning with certain laws for her son, things to do (things to avoid). Following the example handed down from the Lord with the 10 commandments the don'ts (do nots) are given first:

- Do not be a whoremonger
- Do not be a drunkard (along with why not engage in that behavior)?
  » It is not becoming to kings

» It is not becoming to princes (something he will teach his sons)
» Lest they forget God's law (does anybody know that a drunken state impairs one's memory?)

Lest they pervert justice. To pervert is to cause to turn away from what is right, proper, or good. In Job 8:3, the question is asked – Does God pervert justice? In other words, does God twist justice? Does the Almighty twist what is right? *God forbid, God's word means what He said, and says what He means.* Brothers and sisters, every good thing that God created, Satan (our one common enemy) works to pervert. Satan works to twist God's people away from obeying God's word!

Next, she gives the things to do:

Do help such as are unable to plead their own cause in court (the king is to be a public defender of the less fortunate).

Do judge righteous judgment. Brothers and sisters, let me drop this question on you that Apostle Paul asks in 1 Corinthians 6:2 – *Do ye not know that the saints will judge the world?* It takes one that is righteous to judge righteously! Hallelujah! The foundation is laid for us in Matthew 6:33 – *but seek ye first the kingdom of God and His righteousness.* What are the kingdom of God and His righteousness? God's way of doing things! How do we seek God's way of doing things? Isaiah 55:6 reads, *seek ye the Lord while He may be found, call ye upon Him while He is near.* When do we do that brothers and sisters? While we are yet alive! Jeremiah 29:13 reads, *and ye shall seek me, and find me when ye shall search for me with all your heart!* **Back to the Basics!** Jesus in the morning, Jesus at noon, Jesus in the night! Here's a familiar nugget for you – ask and it shall be given unto you, seek and ye shall find, knock and it shall be opened unto you. Where does it begin brothers and sisters? When we a-s-k, ask, seek, knock! Where does it take place? From our hearts to God's heart.

Do plead the cause of the poor.

This is a familiar act of God, getting **back to the basics**, for through Moses, He gave the Israelites – hence, us things not to do and things to do also:

- Do not have other gods before me
- Do not steal
- Do not commit adultery
- Do remember the Sabbath day, to keep it holy
- Do labor six days and do all thy work
- Do honor thy father and thy mother that thy days may be longer upon the land, and so on…

Last, the king's mother gets into the meat of his lesson (and ours) – the birds and bees. She paints the picture of the "model woman". A virtuous woman. Virtuous – pure, chaste. Pure – genuine, true, simple. Chaste – clean, pure and consecrated. It is characteristic of a virgin.

The model woman is morally perfect, invaluable, trustworthy (gaining her husband's confidence), inherently good and true. Ingenious – proficient (labors ceaselessly), thrifty – laborious, dutiful – considerate, versatile – judicious, tireless – healthy, joyful – efficient, watchful – cautious, thrifty – skillful.

The model woman will be about good works of charity – benevolent, in her household she is generous – merciful, fearless – provident, clever at decorating furnishing, refined in taste, and her personal appearance is impeccable. In one of former President Obama's interviews about when he first met the first lady, Michelle, he said "she was crisp". To me, that says, in his eyes, everything he saw about her was tight!

The model woman is respected – she has the respect of her husband:

- He has absolute confidence in her faithfulness
- He knows she will not be a waster; she has no need for spoils of a neighbor to supply his house
- He is blessed by her tireless industry all the days of his life
- He is exalted as a ruler with the elders at the gate
- He praises her virtues and blessings to others

The king's mother moves from the model woman to his woman. Proverbs 31:25-31 lays out the character, diligence, labor, praise and godliness of a woman befitting her son, the character, diligence labor, praise and godliness of a woman befitting to a king! The king's mother conveys to him – my son, your woman should be:

- Dependable – honest
- Confident – hopeful
- Wise – ever active
- An ideal wife and mother
- Honored by her family and the public
- Virtuous
- God fearing – humble
- Deserving – successful

Getting back to the basics!

We, as women of God are to excel all other women in wifehood, motherhood, religion, and industry! Grace of manner is deceitful and beauty of form and features will fade, but the woman who fears the Lord shall be praised! Give such a woman praise and acclaim in the public and render her the fruit of her hands! Women of God, young women, little girls, the king's mother has laid out the character we are to possess in presenting ourselves to the king…. our king. His name is Jesus!!

Proverbs 22:6 tells us, *train up a child in the way he should go, and when he is old he will not depart from it.* As a child, I was trained, like most, to abstain from sex, get a good education, and have children after marriage. These were good values – in line with scripture: 1 Corinthians 16:18 – *flee fornication,* 2 Timothy 2:15 – *study to show thyself approved unto God,* Hebrew 13:4 – *marriage is honorable in all.* Unfortunately, as prophet Isaiah warned in Isaiah 53:6 – *we, like sheep have gone astray, each of us has turned to our own way.*

We as teens, adolescents, and young adults tend to stray from the values instilled in us as children, succumbing to peer pressure. Some of us engage in what's popular (other people's values), although the soft whisper in our ear (heart) lets us know we're doing wrong. Society promotes freedom from constraints. Advertisers entice us with succulent ads of love, safe sex, responsible drinking, and getting an education is always an option, regardless of age, socio-economic status. What is not advertised – consequences of straying; following the values of others. Peer pressure sometimes extends into societal pressure.

What are some of the consequences I experienced resulting from straying away from my values to the values of others? Premarital sex lead to a child before marriage, delaying my getting *a good education*, and returning back to the basics, abstaining from sex, pursuing higher education as I raised my child, later, children, and instilling the core values I was raised to Thank God that delaying is not denying.

God knows our sin nature, waits with open arms for us to return to those values. I am now back on track after returning back to the basics in my journey to find and fulfill my destiny. I believe you will, as I have been able to experience joy and peace, for there is less pressure on us when we get **back to the basics**. Find and fulfill your destiny.

Chapter 6
Learn From The Greats

Michael Jackson (MJ) says in his autobiography to *study the greats and become greater*. This is valuable direction or advice to follow for it goes in line with not re-inventing the wheel, something that has been taught for many, many years. It is the same principle of finding a working model and emulating it until your style, system or way of doing things develops. MJ was blessed to be in the company of many greats in the Motown days when he was a young boy. We too are surrounded by greats. In our world the greats may be parents, grandparents, aunts, uncles, friends, coaches, siblings, teachers, ministers, the list could continue on and on. The greats to emulate could be organizations or business entities for those building similar projects. I was blessed with an Allstate franchise for several years, then decided to go independent as All Peoples, a name I registered and own to date. I modeled All Peoples in the manner I learned as an Allstate franchisee. Principles of practice are basic lessons of business practiced universally, ethics, rules and regulations, licensure and certifications, continuing education requirements, interviewing staff and clients. Hiring laws, staffing the agency, discipline and firing, giving raises and promotions, finding and securing locations, distance proximity of other agencies, setting goals for the business, which was very interesting and enlightening. Goal setting should never end. As we evolve from one level of maturity to the next, setting and achieving goals will never stop.

The journey to find and fulfill your destiny will require studying, learning, and continuous growth. Learning from the greats provides a roadmap to follow. Solomon, the wisest man known, said in Ecclesiastes 1:9, *that which has been done is that which shall be; and that which has been done is that which will be; and there is nothing new under the sun.* In other words, somebody has already done what we're trying to do. We can study what has been done, do our part in making it better, adding to it, and make it greater. It is the same principle we follow in classrooms, and churches learning from teachers, professors, pastors, and chaplains. Learning from the greats paves the way for us to find and fulfill our destiny!

Moving from jack of all trades to master of one

From as far back as I can remember I have worked several jobs simultaneously or worked one or more jobs while going to school for something. Two things happened to me that changed my wayward actions to becoming more focused. The first, by the way, both happened while living in Miami after getting out of the military; I read an article in the Miami Herald where the reporter wrote that he called a residence asking to speak to Dr. Somebody and a child answered the phone. When asked to speak with Dr. Somebody, the child responded with, which one? Right then and there I paused, thought to myself – that will be me one day. I already had the desire of a college education, but had not thought of going all the way with an educational journey. I set the goal then and there I was going to be Dr. Mary Cynthia. Actually, Dr. Cynthia for I don't use the first name, Mary. I envisioned being married to a doctor, I'm a doctor, someone calls my house, one of my daughters answers the phone, when Dr. Whatever is asked for, the response is, which one, and it was a perfect fit. That was the first time I had thoughts that high of myself. That was the first time I saw unlimited possibilities for ME. I had a big dream of accomplishing something that would set me on the track that I felt was mine. I owned that dream and of course as a doctor I would earn enough to support my daughters and me. The next incident came after I started a career in sales. Insurance sales. Selling insurance was my introduction to reading self-help books on motivation and goal-setting, measuring success, overcoming rejection, attending workshops and conferences on those topics. I learned about the universal laws of selling from Brian Tracy on how the *thing you're seeking is seeking you*. I began quoting to people positive affirmations Zig Ziglar's *I'll see you at the top*. My way of thinking, my attitude was becoming for me to never settle for being in the herd, be the thoroughbred, the soaring eagle. People skills are taught in sales, verbal and nonverbal communications. Eye contact while speaking to someone is an indicator of the effectiveness of reaching the person or not. I learned the importance of knowing when to stop talking and listen, a skill that is also crucial when counseling and coaching others. Les Brown taught on the importance of humor and how much better we look when smiling or laughing, *we don't look so homely*. It was during those years I began seeking what I enjoyed doing most, what was I doing better than anything else? What had I been doing and not getting paid for? The answer to each question had three common activities, reading, writing, and talking. In other words, communicating. I decided to develop myself as a speaker and began volunteering to speak whenever I could.

I joined speaking organizations, The National Speakers Association, Toastmasters, Kiwanis International. By joining speaking organizations, I was able to immerse into literature, books, and live events of great speakers. I watched their hand gestures, took note of voice fluctuations in emphasizing important points or facts. I noticed diction and eye contact, facial expressions, and crowd interactions before, during, and after speaking. I was fascinated with the process, and remain so today. That's what MJ did as he watched other great performers, singers, and dancers. He paid attention to the techniques, practiced them, until his style evolved. I emulated great speakers and practiced until my style emerged as a speaker. The evolution has not ended. I will be a lifelong student and professional speaker, and teacher to those watching me. I enrolled in a seminary, which closed its doors mid-stream, but continued seeking The Lord on the type of speaking He would have me to do, and He elevated me to the call of speaking in ministry as a minister. I am blessed to near the end of my journey of becoming Dr. Cynthia, all coursework finished and dissertation in the works.

I actually just thought of a fourth pivotal incident, my daughters, both grown and on their own now, the eldest completed her doctorate three years ago. I started first but while working and she was able to go full time in the military. The youngest is still working on undergrad studies. Although I am still working while completing my doctorate, it is not a jack of all trades scenario, for the activities are related and focused. I am not in survival mode as previously, I am in a Jabez prayer answering blessing. Bruce Wilkinson brought the prayer to everyone's attention with his book on it. The prayer is nestled in 1 Chronicles 4:10, *And Jabez called on the God of Israel, saying, Oh that thou would bless me indeed, and enlarge my coast, and that thine hand might be with me, and that thou would keep me from evil, that it may not grieve me! And God granted him that he requested.* I can see many blessings that have manifested since praying this prayer. My territory or coast has been enlarged, God is blessing me to reach more and more people to serve in all aspects of my life – work, school, church, community, and at large, meaning even while travelling outside my immediate area. It is a prayer that touches every need in life and is short and simple, very easy to commit to memory. It is also an affirmation of stepping outside the box, allowing God to use you according to His will and plans, which are unlimited.

We are living creatures created by a living God, and create living entities which require attention of nurturing, similar to the same nurturing we do with children. Time and attention are necessary and just as children require more as they grow up, develop more interests we spend more on them. Businesses are similar in that as the business grows, more of our time is required. We spend more in additional resources, human and inanimate. This is saying that we hire more staff and purchase more desks, computers, and whatever is needed.

Great business people invest in their businesses, for we must spend money on advertising and the aforementioned resources for success. I also learned from the greats that we must spend money on ourselves. Speakers must be well groomed in outer appearance in addition to being knowledgeable on our topics. The greats take pride in credibility and reputation. We must also take care in our health, physical and mental well being. Covey, another great, named one of the seven habits that we must develop, is to *take time to sharpen the saw to be effective.* It is important to learn from the greats and become greater as we seek to find and fulfill our destiny! As we seek to find and fulfill our destiny, it is important to *learn from the greats, and become greater!*

Chapter 7
Look, Listen, and Leap!

It is not enough to have a desire to serve or help others, we must be attentive to their needs and desires, get educated, seek wise counsel, and take action. I mentioned earlier that I wanted a college education but started a family before it was accomplished. As my eldest daughter got closer to high school, the intensity of need heightened. I remember talking to The

Lord telling Him how I would soon need to help my daughter get her college degree and I still didn't have mine, wasn't earning enough to afford it, and did not want the door closed on her for reasons that I was falling short. I asked The Lord to help me to get my degree now, so that I could help her cheerfully and not regretfully. I took a serious look at my situation, was willing to listen to the inner voice of my heart, and recognize the need for me to leap out on faith with God's help in pursuit of what I believed to be an important step in me being able to find and fulfill my destiny. Crying out in prayer alone would not get it done. I had to take action. This action reminds me of another great woman, the Queen of Sheba, who took action for a situation she was facing. Scripture does not reveal specifics of what she faced but does state that she sought the wisdom of King Solomon and shared all things on her heart. The queen's actions also display an example of reciprocity, in that she did not approach King Solomon with her agenda only in mind. She approached him with humility and resourceful gifts. In other words, she didn't visit to get something only; she came to give something also. It was not a selfish visit. Let's take a look at her visit to the king:

QUEEN OF SHEBA

I Kings 10:1-13 also same account of the queen is given in 2 Chronicles 9:1-12

In Biblical times, the title queen was used as a reigning queen, a queen consort (companion, partner, spouse or mate), chief wife (Esther) or wife of first rank.

QUEEN OF SHEBA is a reigning queen, having royal power and sovereign rule.

SHEBA – a country in Africa or Arabia (named after the grandson of Cush).

V1. This is a political move as a **leader** – comparable to what we have seen in recent presidential debates. Presidential candidates having to prove themselves with hard questions (riddles and complicated sayings).

V2. **Precise steps of a leader**

The queen showed with precise steps that the call to action – look, listen, and leap applies to us all. Although a ruler herself, she paid attention to a leader she felt had knowledge and experience she could learn and grow from. Knowledge and experience she could apply to her kingdom and become more effective as a ruler. The queen was on a quest to find and fulfill her destiny as a great ruler.

- She heard (by commercial interchange (trade route) the name of the Lord accompanied Solomon due to his wisdom.
- She came to prove him with riddles
- She communed with him all that was in her heart
- She saw all his wisdom

- She said it was a true report – the half had not been told
- She gave gifts to him
- She returned to her own country

Queen of Sheba not only came to prove him with hard sayings but also to reward him should he prove to be as she had heard.

Preparation of a leader: the queen came with

- Hard questions
- A very great train of camels that bare spices
- Very much gold
- Many precious stones

V4-5 The queen assessed what she had seen and heard and there was no spirit in her. It all "took her breath away".

- Solomon's wisdom
- The house he built
- Meat at his table
- The sitting of his servants
- The attendance of his ministers
- The apparel of his ministers
- The apparel of his cupbearers
- The ascent by which he went up into the house of the Lord
- *To sum up what the queen saw in two words were wisdom & prosperity!*

The actions of a leader: the queen gave Solomon

- 120 talents of gold at $29,085 in their dollars would be $3,490,200 in our dollars.
- Spices & precious stones. These could've been equal in value to the gold.

Queen of Sheba is a strong, successful, wise woman that sets the bar for greatness. She reigned in a time it was not most popular for women to be in leadership or power. She shows an excellent example of approaching someone of great power without intimidation. In addition to that her approach with a caravan of servants and riches showed the king that she too was resourceful. Similar visits occur today in our political world. Gifts are exchanged between leaders on visits as a symbol of respect and mutual greatness. Leaders all over the world look at what one another is doing, listen to what is going on in other countries, and leap into action as they deem necessary. The forefathers of the great United States left England to find and fulfill their destiny away from the constraints of British law. We enjoy the liberties today resulting from their vision and action.

This is your season

The urgency of now

YOUR SEASON

I saw a clip recorded during former President Obama's campaign where he mentioned that Dr. King talked about *the swift urgency of now*. I pondered on that, prayed to The Lord for guidance and clarity. I am completing my dissertation in fulfilling the last requirement leading to graduating a doctoral program. It is very arduous and many, many emotions are experienced. I think this process is really showing me what I am made of, so to speak. I began experiencing a sense of un-accomplishment. The process is long and slow moving for me, so I began looking back on my life's pursuits. I had completed my undergraduate degree, Masters degree, and it was all academic. I wondered, what does the creative side of me have to offer? Surely there is a creative side to me. After all, I learned to sew at a young age and did that as a means of clothes for myself in high school. I played the clarinet in band. I wrote poetry in my diary. I used to talk like Donald Duck and make my siblings laugh. Those activities were not continued through the years, so I felt I wasn't being creative. My job is administrative; I do not create graphics or anything like that, so I wanted something creative to add to my repertoire. I was thinking of exploring the creative side of me after graduating with my doctorate, but the words, *urgency of now* resonated in me. In asking The Lord to show me His glory, I also said to Him that I would like to serve the masses. I have been speaking The Word of God in churches since the 1990s in each city I've lived, each church I've been a member. Although it is fulfilling serving my local church, there was a desire in me that it was not enough. One afternoon, I saw a Facebook invite to a session on writing a book that matters. I accepted, attended, prayed and The Lord spoke to me to move forward. There was no need for me to wait until after graduation. He wants me to serve the masses NOW. I reflected back on how quickly things were moving in my life since asking God to show me His glory, how many more people were being placed in my path for prayer, people were encouraging me to continue preaching for The Lord brought understanding to them through my messages. I am so very grateful for this opportunity to pen the words The Lord is pouring into me to share with you and be an example that no matter what life throws at you, God is true to his word all the time.

Of course, the enemy showed up with doubt, blank moments when the words should've been flowing from my heart onto the pages, but the more God shows you to do, and you step out, the more important it is to stay in His presence and not let thoughts of when I graduate, when I retire, when my children grow up, or anything else get in the way. When The Lord gives the assignment to you, the time is now! The season is yours!

I could say to you this is **your season** to (You fill in the blank) or I could ask do you need to **season your**? (Again, you fill in the blank).

It's all in perception and reception! I read or heard a story some years ago of a man with four sons that he sent out at different times to observe a fruit tree and told them to return and report how the tree looked. The first went out in summer and reported beautiful blossoms on the tree. The second went out during fall and reported the tree was full of ripe fruit. The third went out during winter and saw an old ugly bare tree. The fourth went out during spring and saw green buds on the tree. The report back to their father was how each perceived the tree. I receive the fall ripe fruit as a harvest and the green buds of spring as newness, a promise of something to come. I had to perceive my finished book, me speaking to God's people all over the world to encourage myself to continue. I had to receive that God is with me always, even to the end of the world, for there were times it seemed quite dismal. I studied The Word of God on seasons in Ecclesiastes, penned by the wisest man known, Solomon.

Solomon, the preacher begins the third chapter of Ecclesiastes with a statement,

*To everything there is a **season** and a time to every purpose under the heaven*, and the statement continues through eight verses and ends in the ninth verse with a question,

What profit has he that work in that wherein he labour?

Our focus is on Seasons of Life – **YOUR SEASON** or is it Life of Seasons – **SEASON**

YOUR LIFE? The second question you may be asking, do I need to season my prayer life, do I need to season my time spent studying God's Word, do I need to season my …, well, you get the picture.

To man, there are four **seasons:**

- Summer
- Fall
- Winter
- Spring

To God, there are twenty-eight **seasons:**

- To be born
- Die
- Plant
- Pluck up
- Kill
- Heal
- Breakdown

- Build up
- Weep
- Laugh
- Mourn
- Dance
- Cast away stones
- Gather stones
- Embrace
- Refrain from embracing
- Get, buy or acquire
- Lose, or take a loss
- Keep things
- Cast away things
- Rend, or tear
- Sew, or join together
- Keep silent
- Speak your mind
- Love
- Hate, or make preference
- Make war
- Make peace

Integrating **YOUR SEASON** with God's **season** would encompass:

- SUMMER – A period of maturing powers. Maturing (fully developed). Build up, Weep, Laugh, Mourn, Dance, Cast away stones, Gather stones.
- FALL – A period of maturity or incipient decline. A period of maturity or the inception (beginning) decline. Embrace, Refrain from embracing, Get, buy or acquire, Lose, or take a loss, Keep things, Cast away things, Rend, or tear.
- WINTER – Period of inactivity or decay. No activity or gradual decline in strength, soundness or prosperity. Sew, or join together, Keep silent, Speak your mind, Love, hate or make preference, Make war, Make peace

- SPRING – A time or **season** of growth or development. Be born, Die, Plant, Pluck up, kill, Heal, Break down.

All of us experience God's twenty-eight seasons wrapped up in man's four in our lives, in our Christian walk. Would you agree with me that SUMMER is a great **season?** A time wherein brothers and sisters build up one another by witnessing, praying and worshipping together, laugh, dance, cast away stone (laying aside every weight)? A time when all is well and we can declare that Life is beautiful!!

Would you agree with me that FALL is a good **season?** A time wherein brothers and sisters can embrace our harvest without apologizing for our prosperity? Embracing the many souls the Lord allowed us to witness to and seeing them busy in the ministry. Not complaining about the relationships we were able to tear away from and keep moving higher and higher in God's

Kingdom! Maturing in the wisdom of the Lord by planting seeds in others preparing for another **season.** After all, it's not about us and only what we do for Christ will last.

Would you agree with me that WINTER, regardless of its challenges, is STILL a nice **season?** We may sometimes find ourselves in a slump…not praying as much as we did in our glorious summer, resulting in us not bridling our tongues, speaking our minds, making war. In the gradual decline in strength, we may not always join together; but God, in His infinite mercy still shows His Love for us so that we may move forward into yet another **season!** He will allow us to see a situation that will prevent our winter from turning into a blizzard, for bad does not have to go to worse.

Finally, would you agree with me that SPRING is the **season** we all love? A time to be born anew? Pluck up the old man so that he may die? Break down barriers that have kept us from being all we can be in the Lord? Heal old wounds, hurts and sorrows and plant green buds filled with promise for the future!!

What profit has he that works in that wherein he labours? What profit have you for all your witnessing to sinners? What profit have you for all your prayers for others? What profit have you for fasting and sacrificing for the Kingdom's sake? The profit is doing The Will of God, spreading love and sharing The Gospel so people have hope and God gets glory.

Our Lord and Saviour Jesus Christ was hung high and stretched wide on Calvary's cross for you and me. He died and rose again in the season of SPRING for us to be redeemed to the FATHER. He that believeth shall have everlasting life!

Praise the Lord for it is **YOUR SEASON** – season your life to your taste. Find and fulfill your destiny!

Chapter 8
Overcoming Melancholy

I was experiencing another spiritual warfare attack this morning. I had feelings of falling short and getting embarrassed by not having as much written as my perceived expectation, sent a post to my mentor expressing the feelings going on. Of course, she returned a very positive response that I am okay just where I am, which is God's way of showing me – I already told you I will never leave, never forsake you. Immediately, my spirit was pricked that I've just been given another chapter. Of course the enemy is going to show up trying to block you from doing God's will in getting His word out. Look how Paul was shipwrecked three times while on mission trips. What made me think I would go through this process on a bed of ease? I tell people frequently when experiencing attacks of the enemy, God's got you! Of course our enemy comes but to kill, steal, and destroy; but God. Hallelujah! I must take a praise break right here and now. Lord thank you for showing me your glory for even in this you are doing exceedingly above what I thought and asked. I love you and thank you for first loving me, amen. I am literally trembling in the presence of Him, hands shaking on the keyboard.

I am reminded of something I heard a minister say on the drive into work this morning on our eyes, likened to binoculars.

With binoculars when looking through the little part and seeing through the big part, what we are looking at is magnified; but when looking through the big part, seeing through the little part, what we see is minimized. Hallelujah! I had a moment of distorted emotions, seeing this writing through the big part, perceiving myself falling short, falling into a place of doubt. God forbid. Perception is a powerful tool the enemy can use against us if we are not conscious of his devices and get Godly counsel. Depression, despair, desperation, if not honed in, can lead us down a slippery slope. Satan showed up while I was writing the section on renewing our minds, changing negative thoughts to positive thoughts. The presence was so strong that I was in a place that all I could do was lie before The Lord in prayer and praise. At one point I got up from the computer, got a blanket and pillow, lying on the floor in front of my desk quietly for a time, allowing The Lord to minister to me. It wore me out! This current attack took place in my office at work. I now realize that my inner author showed up because God is going to finish this work He has started in me getting this information out to you so I may serve.

I have learned over the years that the *worse things can happen at the worse times,* known as Murphy's Law. As you seek to find and fulfill your destiny, obstacles will come from every direction. You must stay focused, committed, have fun, and remain steadfast to ensure that you find and fulfill your destiny!

Fear must go now

Unleash your passion

Like being You

Follow the signs

Instill your values

Learn from the greats

Look, listen, and Leap!

Find and fulfill your destiny!

Acknowledgments

All praise and glory goes to our Lord and Savior, Jesus the Christ, the Anointed One. I am grateful for the opportunity to share my life experiences to you, readers of this book. Training for this endeavor began with My aunt, Rosa, who tutored me during my pre-school years, which led to literacy before starting school. Miss Ellen, my first Sunday School teacher, who would have me read to the class because we were all pre-schoolers but I alone could read, count, and help her.

I was blessed by Ms. Shaw, my elementary school cafeteria manager at C.A. Moore, who taught me to sell and be responsible for money.

She trusted me implicitly and introduced me to business. Ms. Minus nurtured me into leadership in the fifth grade by giving me teacher assistant responsibilities as a class leader. Mr. Grant, who introduced me to the clarinet in the sixth grade by showing me a picture of one. Bishop Gordon, who saw something in me as a speaker and business woman, and prayed for God to give me a double portion of what he had – a man well respected and sought after as a great preacher.

I am grateful to my high school classmate and fellow minister, Pastor Collins, who called on me multiple times to speak at his church in my early years of preaching. Pastor Southall, who opened his church doors to me to preach. Rev. Ingram and Rev. Burks, who supported me as a minister and businesswoman while in my hometown, Ft. Pierce, FL. I thank Pastor Patz for the love and support while serving in Gainesville. Thank you Rev. Jules and Ida

Smith, the Rising Star Missionary Baptist Church family in Denver for all your love, support, and encouragement.

I am blessed to have the most patient, kind, efficient publisher in Morgan James Publishing. Their team got me through the book process with ease and pleasantry – many thanks! Special Thanks to David Hancock, CEO & Founder for believing in me and my message. To my Author Relations Manager, Tiffany Gibson, thanks for making the process seamless and easy. Many more thanks to everyone else, but especially Jim Howard, Bethany Marshall, and Nickcole Watkins.

I am very grateful for my birth in the land of opportunity, the United States of America. May God bless all who have served and those continuing to serve and keep this land safe and enjoyable.

God bless us all, and God bless America, amen. I love you!

About the Author

Cynthia is a contract specialist for the Department of Veterans Affairs (VA) in Denver, Colorado. As a contract specialist, she is a buyer for the federal government purchasing  goods and services for VA hospitals and out-patient community-based clinics serving the nation's veterans located in Oklahoma, Colorado, Utah, Montana, and Wyoming. She is a veteran, having served in the U.S. Air Force.

She has a Doctor of Education, concentration in Organizational Leadership, a Master of Arts in Public Administration, and a Bachelor's in Organizational Management.

Cynthia lives in Colorado and is an Associate Minister at Rising Star Missionary Baptist Church in Denver, Colorado.

Thank You

Thank you for reading! I hope that after going through these pages you now feel confident in taking steps to find and fulfill your destiny.

If you're looking to take the practice in this book even deeper, write to me at anononsenseyou@gmail.com.